KU-441-103

FUN TO DRAW

Sharks

AND OTHER UNDERWATER CREATURES!

ROBERT AINSWORTH

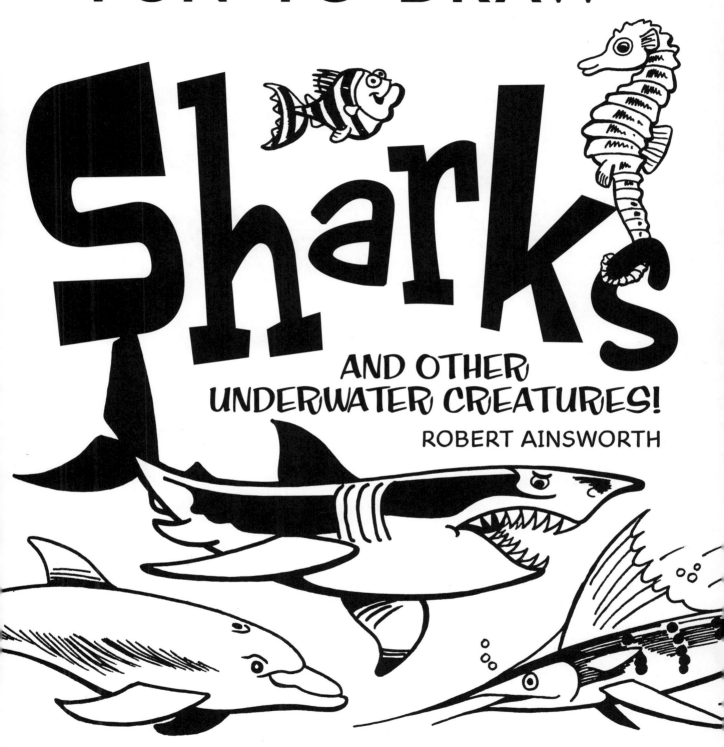

SCHOLASTIC

DEDICATED TO
MY PET GOLDFISH, WHO KEPT ME
COOL WHILE I WROTE THIS BOOK.

Scholastic Australia Pty Limited
PO Box 579 Gosford NSW 2250
ABN 11 000 614 577
www.scholastic.com.au

Part of the Scholastic Group
Sydney • Auckland • New York • Toronto • London • Mexico City
• New Delhi • Hong Kong • Buenos Aires • Puerto Rico

Published by Scholastic Australia in 2011.
Text and illustrations copyright © Robert Ainsworth, 2011.

All rights reserved. No part of this publication may be reproduced or transmitted in any form or by any means, electronic or mechanical, including photocopying, recording, storage in an information retrieval system, or otherwise, without the prior written permission of the publisher, unless specifically permitted under the Australian Copyright Act 1968 as amended.

National Library of Australia Cataloguing-in-Publication entry

Author:	Ainsworth, Robert, 1951-
Title:	Fun to draw sharks and other underwater creatures / Robert Ainsworth.
ISBN:	9781741696332 (pbk.)
Target Audience:	For primary school age.
Subjects:	Drawing—Technique—Juvenile literature.
	Marine animals in art—Juvenile literature.
	Aquatic animals—Juvenile literature.
Dewey Number:	743.6

Printed in China by WKT.

10 9 8 7 6 5 4 3 2 1   11 12 13 14 15 / 0

CONTENTS

ABOUT THIS BOOK

SHARKS CAN BE PRETTY **SCARY**—BUT WE'RE GOING TO KEEP THEM AT A SAFE DISTANCE... AT THE ENDS OF OUR PENCILS!
I'M GOING TO SHOW YOU HOW TO **DRAW** SHARKS, AND LOTS OF OTHER UNDERWATER CREATURES.
SO TAKE A DEEP BREATH...

AND LET'S **DIVE!**

HAVE *FUN!*

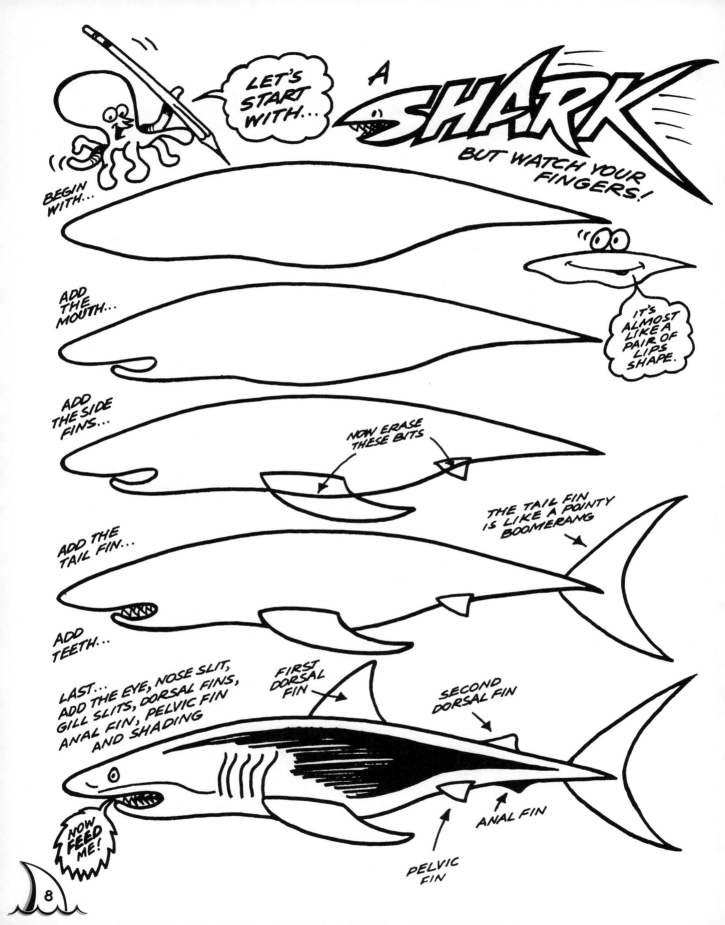

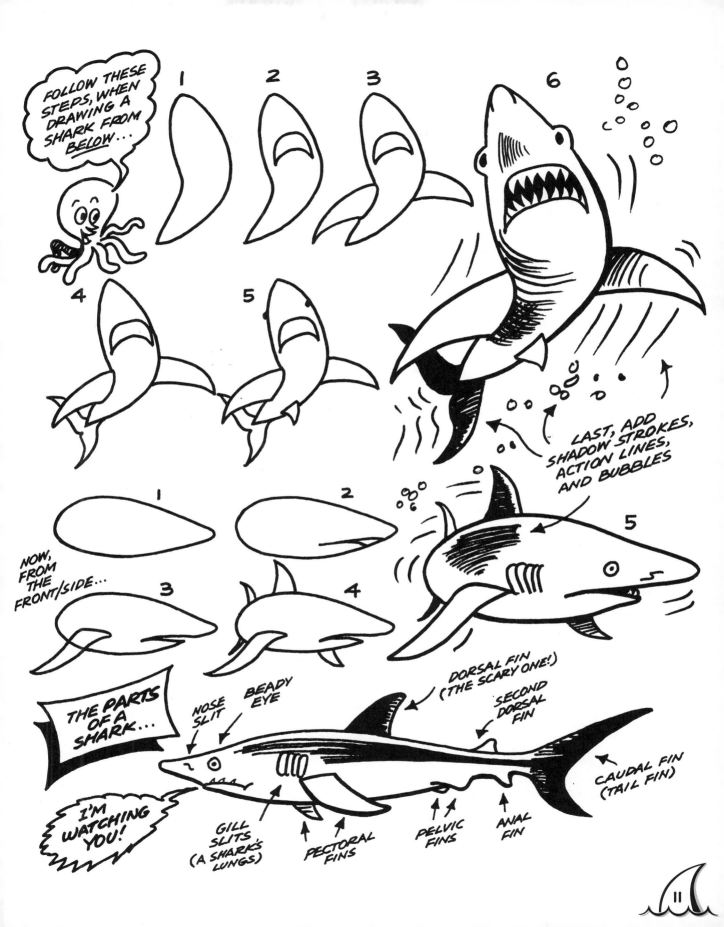

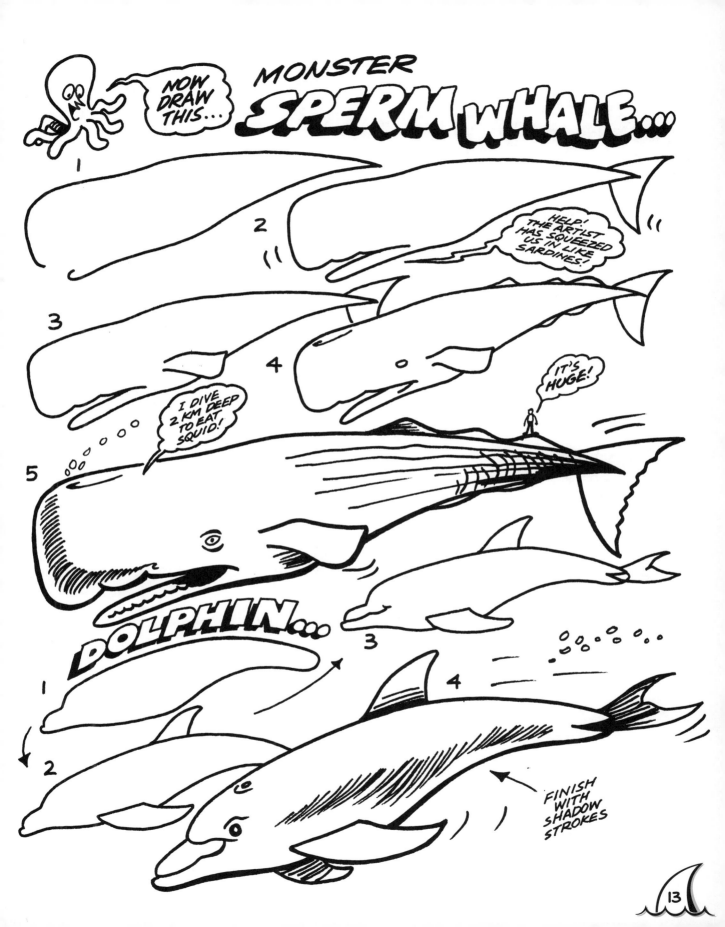

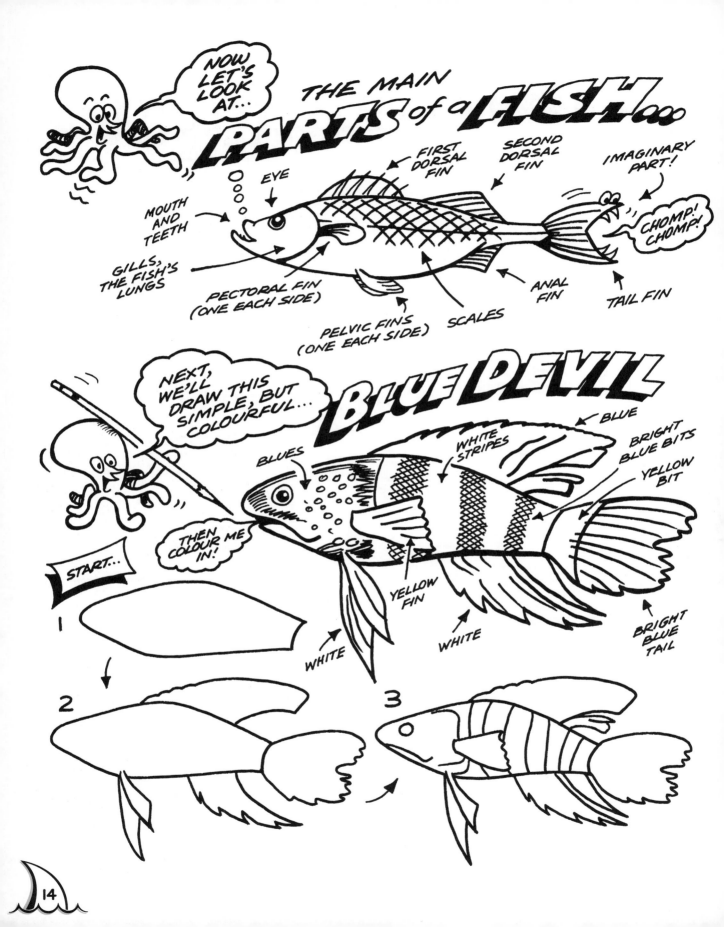

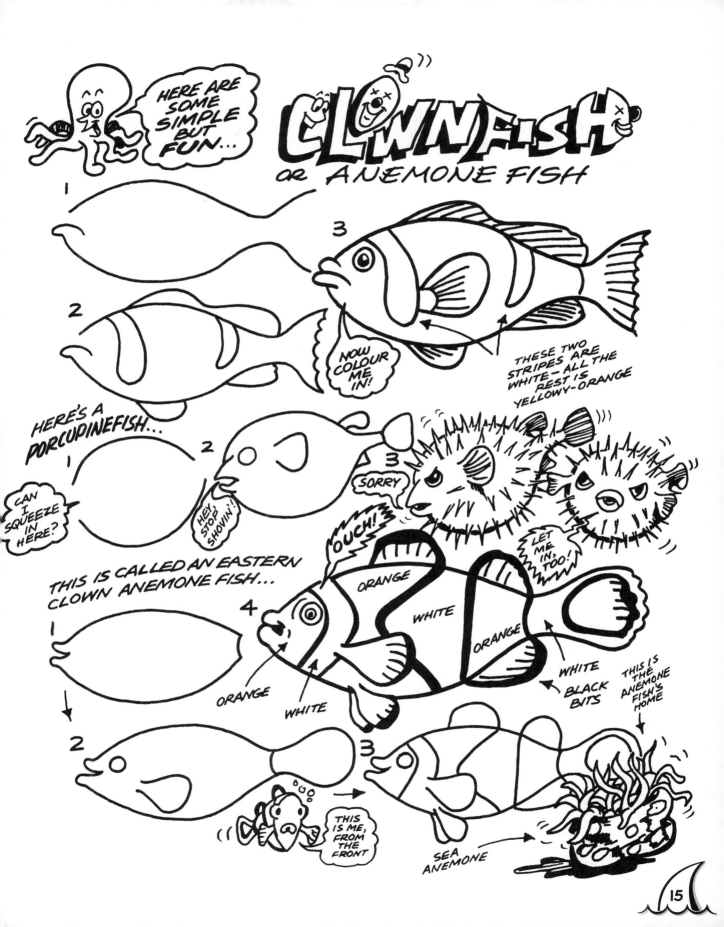

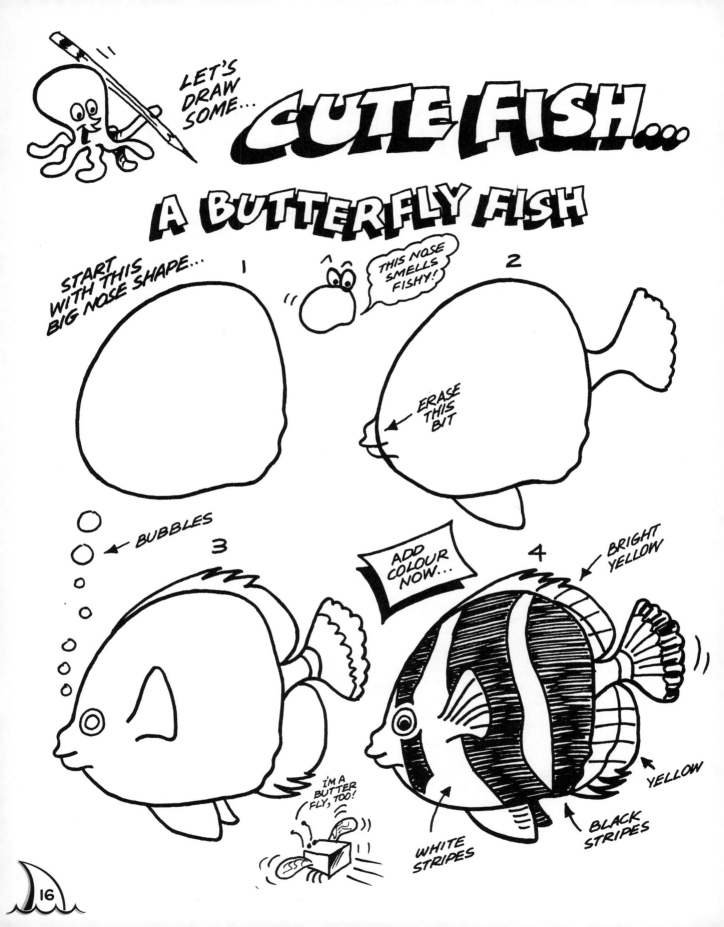

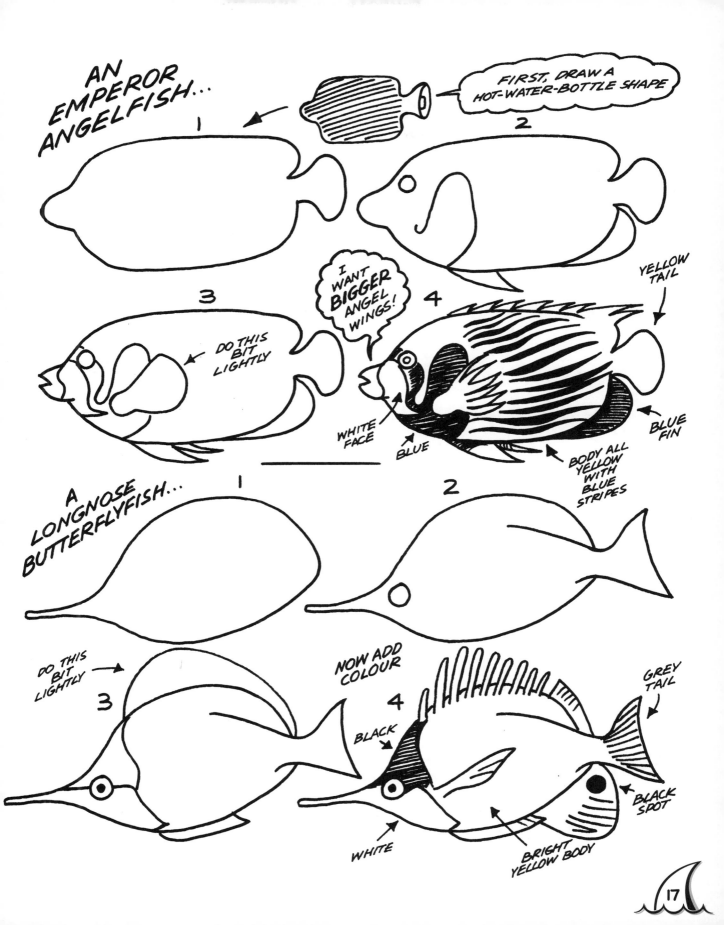

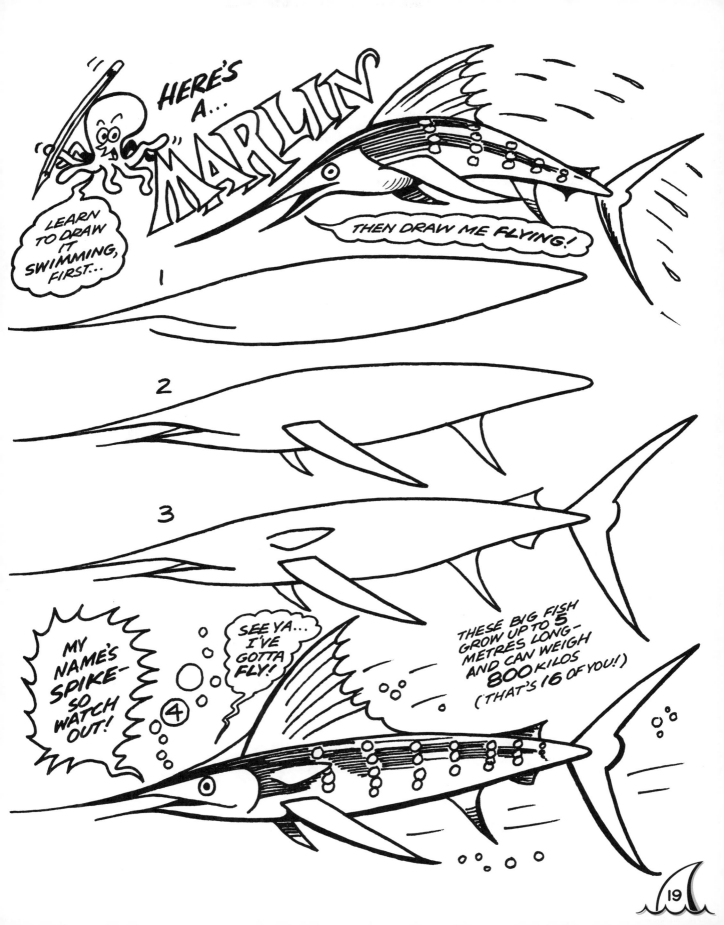

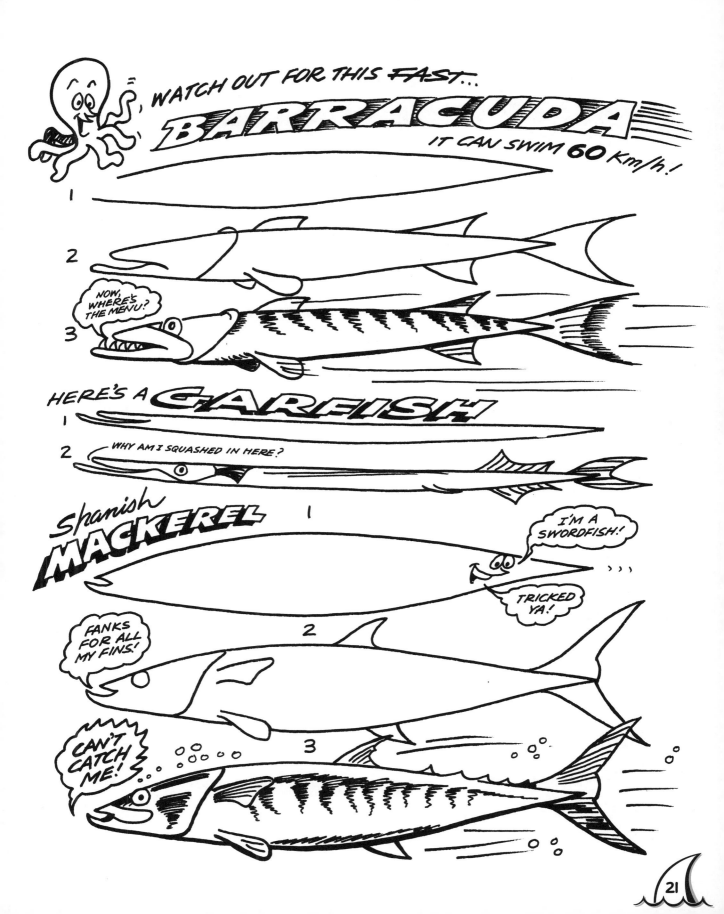

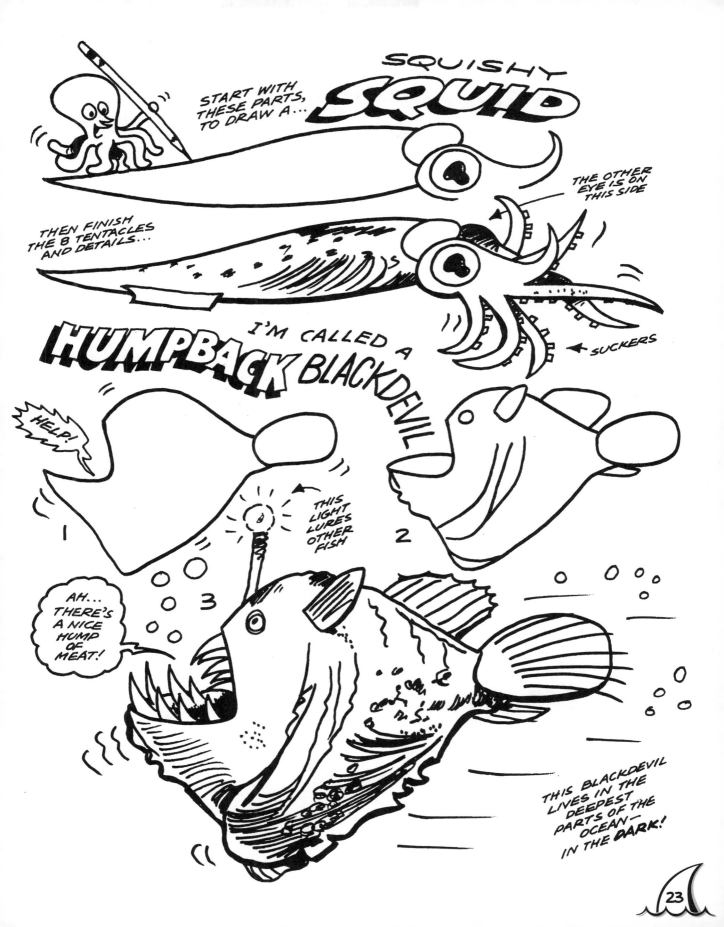

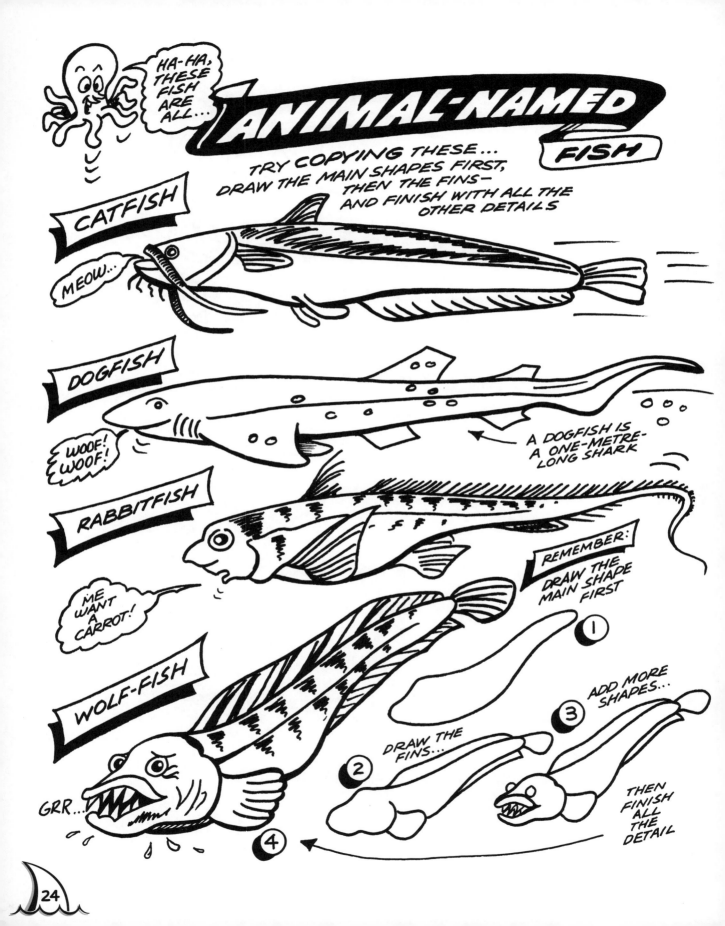

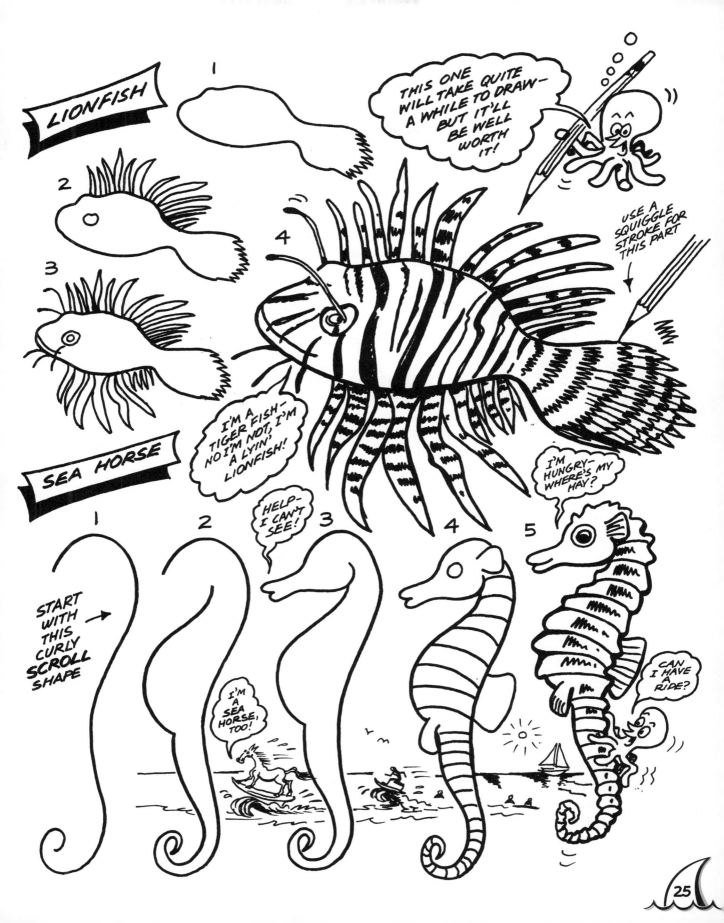

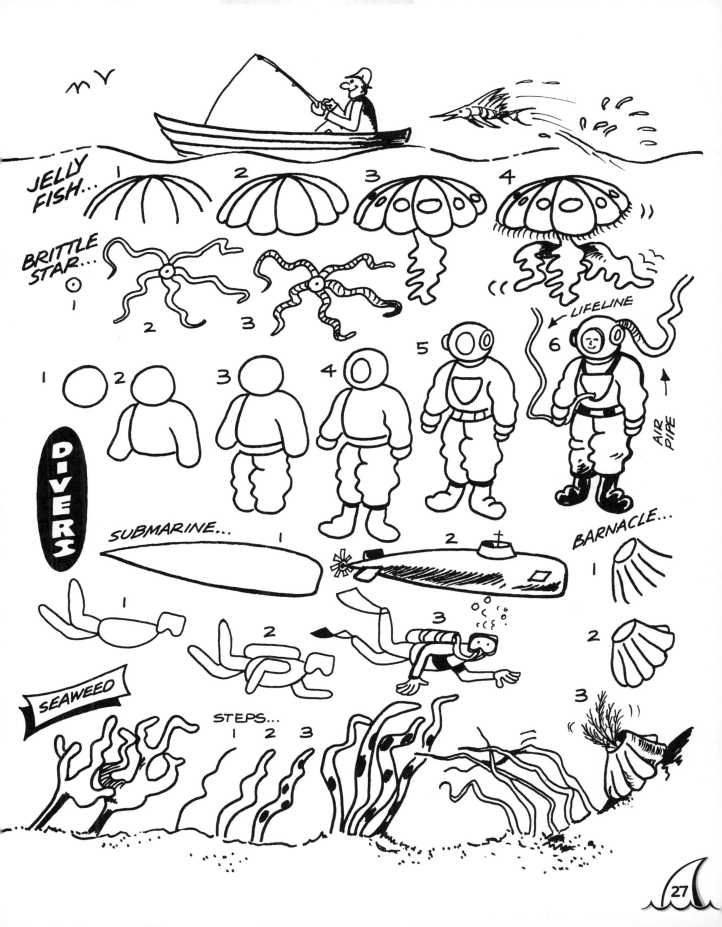

JELLY FISH... 1 2 3 4

BRITTLE STAR... 1 2 3

DIVERS 1 2 3 4 5 6 LIFELINE AIR PIPE

SUBMARINE... 1 2 3

BARNACLE... 1 2 3

SEAWEED STEPS... 1 2 3

27